TRANSACTION HISTORIES

KUHL HOUSE POETS

edited by Mark Levine and Emily Wilson

TRANSACTION HISTORIES

* * *

poems by

DONNA STONECIPHER

University of Iowa Press, Iowa City

University of Iowa Press, Iowa City 52242
Copyright © 2018 by Donna Stonecipher
www.uipress.uiowa.edu
Printed in the United States of America

Design by Ashley Muehlbauer

The University of Iowa Press is a member of Green
Press Initiative and is committed to preserving natural
resources.

Printed on acid-free paper

ISBN 978-1-60938-602-3 (pbk)
ISBN 978-1-60938-603-0 (ebk)

Cataloging-in-Publication data is on file with the
Library of Congress.

CONTENTS

PERSIAN CARPET I

    Persian Carpet 1 3

    Persian Carpet 2 6

    Persian Carpet 3 9

LANDSCAPE AND PORTRAIT 13

TRANSACTION HISTORIES 17

    Transaction History 1 19

    Transaction History 2 22

    Transaction History 3 25

    Transaction History 4 28

    Transaction History 5 31

    Transaction History 6 34

LANDSCAPE AND PORTRAIT 37

ENZYKLOPÄDIE DES UNGESCHMACKS 41

    Enzyklopädie des Ungeschmacks 1 .43

    Enzyklopädie des Ungeschmacks 2 46

    Enzyklopädie des Ungeschmacks 3 49

LANDSCAPE AND PORTRAIT 53

FOUND TO BE BORROWED FROM
SOME MATERIAL APPEARANCE . . . . ·57

Found to Be Borrowed from Some Material Appearance 1 59

Found to Be Borrowed from Some Material Appearance 2 62

Found to Be Borrowed from Some Material Appearance 3 65

Found to Be Borrowed from Some Material Appearance 4 68

Found to Be Borrowed from Some Material Appearance 5 . . . . ·71

Found to Be Borrowed from Some Material Appearance 6 . . . . ·74

LANDSCAPE AND PORTRAIT . . . . ·77

SNOW SERIES 81

Snow Series 1 83

Snow Series 2 86

Snow Series 3 89

"Arbeiten und nicht verzweifeln"
(Keep working, and do not despair)

—BERTOLT BRECHT,
Threepenny Opera, 1928
(adapted from Thomas Carlyle,
"Work and despair not,"
from a letter to George Peacock,
1844)

PERSIAN CARPET

PERSIAN CARPET 1

1.

Months after the breakup, she wondered, how long into the future am I going to keep longing to go back into the past? There was one lock out there, somewhere, iconic in its escutcheon, velvet in its machinery, and fistfuls and fistfuls of keys. On other days there were locks upon locks in rows as in a locksmith's dream, and one key so slippery it kept falling out of her hand into the sky, floating up into the deeps.

2.

The past with its black plastic perfections, its ashtrays and princess telephones. She woke up and mentally listed the pleasures awaiting her: sex, bath, French toast. Or perhaps: sex, French toast, bath. Or, she *used* to wake up and mentally list the pleasures awaiting her. What's past is never past, but moves from room to room in the blue honeycomb of the brain, or blooms in domes that crown the fretted space of her thinking.

3.

In the photograph there were long rows of hooded horses, their eyes like great dark romantic marbles glistening out into the unromantic crowds. One must "break" a horse to tame it. She wanted to banish and punish and fin   ish the past, but the future kept vanishing out of her grasp. The policeman had a soft spot for the procuress, the senator for the chestnut. Too often it seemed her only esprit was l'esprit de l'escalier.

4.

Like the real black swan that fell in love with the plastic black swan-shaped boat and refused to leave "her," even over the winter, in Germany. She read about the swans in a newspaper while sitting on an airplane and   wishing she could get all the way to her destination by speeding down the runway, that the plane would just keep violently hurtling her forward and never, ever lift off.

5.

The island where no cars were allowed was crisscrossed by "broken" horses ferrying
tourists to and from the decommissioned lighthouse. Inside the lighthouse was a blue dome they
could only glimpse through a broken window.   One tourist had an abandoned
honeycomb in his luggage. The past was a Persian carpet arabesquing into the future, losing
her in the ornamental present.

6.

The portrait of the dethroned demagogue had been put out on the sidewalk in the rain
The useless coins filled an old porcelain teacup printed with a skeleton key. She lay in bed
wanting to cut the past out of her body like a   cancer, to strangle its power with fasts
The black plastic swan-boat bobbed gently on the lake as the real black swan glided next to it, the
cynosure of enduring adoration.

PERSIAN CARPET 2

1.

The old bespectacled teacher asked his young bespectacled pupils to imagine what history might look like written by the losers. His star student stared abstractedly out the window, reliving every detail of the previous eve   ning, when she'd had sex for the first time. Touring the foreign city, they were struck by all the obelisks commemorating men who'd fallen in a war they'd never heard of.

2.

It happened at the garden in Normandy in which every flower ever mentioned in Shakespeare had been planted by a solitary gardener who barked at you when you stepped on a blue primrose by mistake. But you knew   that just beyond the garden lay the sea, full of its own blue mistakes, its own glowering gardeners and flowering compendia, and you laughed in the gardener's piqued face.

3.

The only thing on TV that night was an interview with a childlike Leni Riefenstahl aged 100. The only thing on the radio was a reportage on the diseases of the seven seas. The dark streets were deserted, though the neon glo   be revolving slowly on its rooftop axis looked like it would slowly revolve off into some more magnanimous galaxy before the endless night came to some kind of end.

4.

But were their aims so divergent, really, the stargazer and the navel-gazer? Land-locked, she sent frantic mental SOSs to the sea. O she missed its dispassion disdaining her abandon, its translucent sand-crabs scrabbling toward   the gullets of the seagulls, its neritic plumes salting crescive shorelines, the shells and the fragments of shells and the fragments of the fragments of shells.

5.

Another man's obsession with Shakespeare brought a cage with two starlings over to America on a boat, which led to the greatest avian invasion of the century. Couldn't one man have been content with one starling? The   starlings whose dark feathers' gold flecks go snowy in winter, as if snow and gold were dialectical, as if she had opened her gold locket and found it full of snow.

6.

He read history books late into the night and felt like a winner, while she wrote tear stained elegies downstairs alone chain-smoking unfiltered cigarettes, happy that the damage she could do to her body began to match the   damage that had been done to her soul. The starlings nested in the eaves of the old Queen Annes, the old Georgians and Victorians gently rotting in heartland towns.

7.

For years, the man thought that "Persian carpet" *meant* "magic carpet." Which is why, years later, he lined his apartment with such carpets and why, years after that, he broke up with a girlfriend who spilled whiskey on a partic   ularly beautiful pale blue one in the hall. On one wall there was a portrait of Sacco, on the opposite wall a portrait of Vanzetti, and underneath him: seventeen floors.

8.

And the floating ocean of plastic in the upper Pacific Ocean, twice the size of Texas, floated there by all accounts with extreme decorum, reproaching no one, sufficient society unto itself, the zenith of peacefulness, quietly   dilating day by day. From the lookout tower the guide pointed out the bombed steeple that had been left there, jagged and verdigris, in the middle of the rebuilt city.

9.

Damage. Wasn't that the skeleton key? Damage. Darker than the starling's estival feathers, darker than the whiskey stain spreading across the carpet, darker than eaves, than attics, than cellars, than the interiors of damaged   steeples. He let the screen door slam shut as he walked out into the garden to pick four o'clocks and foxgloves, unaware of the poison using beauty for its sepaloid ends.

PERSIAN CARPET 3
(FOR SARAH)

I.

She walked with her seven-year-old niece over the "skybridge" and then through the business "park." Suspended in the sky she looked down at the river, the lake, the freeway and knew what perpendicular longing the sky   does anything but abridge. Was it the deer or the decoy, bounding silver-footed through the trees? He admired the reproduction Greek temple set on the hill.

2.

The psychologist said mildly to his client: I see you've lived in an awful lot of different places. So are you running toward something, or away from something? The client reclined deeper into the divan. The lecturing British   jeweler with Lebanese ancestry was building a watertight case via slide show that the whole of Victorian ornament had been viaducted from the Orient.

9

3.

Nothing terrifies the book like the speed-reader. It was getting harder and harder to find a greenfield. We had lain down for a spell on the Persian carpet to begin woolgathering *les neiges d'antan*. She asked him to please push his   signet ring into the block of wax placed in her soul by Mnemosyne. He thought gleefully of the day when this civilization would exist only as pot fragments.

4.

There are more Victorian houses in San Francisco than in all of England. There have never been more than three types of columns. Two days after her daughter was born, her childless aunt died. Nothing terrifies the book like the   shelf. The librarian was both angel and fallen angel, shelving and shelving. The client liked the psychologist, but knew things really *would* be better in the next city.

5.

What was it like? — It was like hearing a foghorn while deep inland. She lay in the cool dark with her heart pounding, thinking: Soon on my block of wax there won't be any unsignetted space. It was like spending all day at the Ger   man Valhalla, which had been modeled on the French Panthéon, which had been modeled on the Roman Pantheon, which had been modeled on the Greek Parthenon.

6.

She walked hand-in-hand with her seven-year-old niece to the walled garden's digital rose mallows. Nothing terrifies the book like the moving box. The crystal palace's windows were broken. Through frayed fronds the girl   glimpsed the deer's brown glass eye. Wasn't the worst proxy in this ersatz world the artificial flower? The bombyx agreed. (But the polyurethane fern demurred.)

LANDSCAPE

AND

PORTRAIT

LANDSCAPE

(JACOB VAN RUYSDAEL, ZWINGER, DRESDEN, MID-1600S)

Six incidences of landscape arranged in two rows of three, arrangements of arrangements
of nature haloed in velvet oval mats goldenly contained, ovals suggestive of ponds
possibly lurking among the luxuriously dark copses

PORTRAIT

Three container ships packed
with household garbage from France
depart Rotterdam at 12:13 p.m.
bound for India

TRANSACTION HISTORIES

TRANSACTION HISTORY 1

1.

They walked around in the foreign city looking for someplace to have dinner: there was an Italian restaurant, an Indian restaurant, a French restaurant, a Vietnamese restaurant, and a Thai restaurant. Just like in their own city. And in every city they'd ever been to. There were some hungers no restaurant could quiet or curb or quell, and she'd walk out even hungrier than she'd gone in.

2.

Sometimes — we couldn't deny it — life surprised us, presenting us with a sheep in sheep's clothing or a wolf in wolf's clothing. But even this surprise would turn out to be, in the end, a wolf in sheep's clothing, for we would thenceforth mistrust our mistrust, upon which we had come to build our houses. There were only two kinds of birds left in the neighborhood: seagulls and starlings.

3.

The light in the sky was *bleu mourant* — "dying blue" — a term for a particular shade of powder blue he'd learned while working in an antiques shop one summer. When his girlfriend left him that winter, he went around in the snow saying how all the blood in his heart had turned *bleu mourant* overnight. And his heart had turned into an antique, for now it had carnal knowledge of time.

4.

From below, the snow looked like it had been on its way for centuries. People from the small towns dreamed of driving into the city to have their choice of Italian, Indian, Thai, Vietnamese, or French restaurants, but people from the city dreamed of driving to the small town's one restaurant with its three choices of entrée and its view of the derelict Greek Revival library across the street.

5.

Under the *bleu mourant* sky, the sad woman said, "When I wake up at night, I'm like a self-destructive squid, shooting the ink of melancholy into my own heart." Her interlocutor answered: Nec piscatorem piscis amare potest. The small town's populace had long been bitterly divided into those who called the town's main body of water a small lake, and those who called it a large pond.

6.

After dark, people gave the antiques stores a wide berth. As he slid behind the wheel of his black Subaru to drive home to dinner, he tried to remember the last time he'd truly had an appetite. Every last Christmas ornament on the tree had been made in China. Perhaps it was time to reinstate the humble popcorn garland, the gingerbread house. Perhaps it was time, once again, to eat Christmas.

7.

The antiques owed what value they had to those people who believed that objects could give them carnal knowledge of incarnate time. Some countries were winners and some losers in the cosmopolitan restaurant sweepstakes. There were, for example, no Norwegian restaurants in the cities. There was a hunger that just got hungrier and hungrier. *Unquellable,* nodded the self-destructive squid.

8.

The city-dwellers found that they would regularly sleep peacefully through a succession of sirens, garbage trucks, and trains — only to be awakened by the small barking of a faraway dog. Her secret inner structuralist was delighted when her daily errands took her to the department store, where she'd find the sum total of the material world organized and taxonomized down to the last hazelnut.

9.

"The fish cannot love the fisherman" implies that the fish has tried. Notice no one asks if the fisherman can love the fish. There was one hunger hungrier than any other: hunger without appetite. Some small towns on the peninsula now consisted only of a few rows of antiques stores. When the city people left the cities, all they really wanted was to acquire reminders of incarnadine time.

TRANSACTION HISTORY 2

1.

The dark-haired gardener said, I started to sleep better at night when I moved into an apartment across the street from an art museum. Knowing that, hundreds of years after the fact, a green-eyed merchant still looked out aloof from a fur coat, a butterfly still perched on a pomegranate next to a skull, and a blue view of distant hills still hovered behind an annunciation scene with a stunned Mary calmed me down in the deepest unlocked vault of my being.

2.

Certain people were starting to find the sun oppressive, filling the world with its idio-syncratic version of reality as it did day after day. Never mind that it was summer. Looking back through her notebook, she saw that she'd written down "The architects say to the doctors, at least you can bury your mistakes" at least three times in the past year. In 2010, the visiting Chilean president wrote "Deutschland über alles" in the German president's guestbook.

3.

As the city densified, they found themselves looking for non-places. They kept getting obsessed with filing cabinets. They were bewitched by the debt spiral. There still seemed to be some cups in the cupboard, but there were no more gloves in the glove compartment, and hadn't been any in years. One night she found herself sitting in a house high on a hill with spectacular views, but in the dark, the only thing she could see in the windows was herself.

4.

The famous artist told us that he had never slept better in his life than the year he lived in a house opposite a zoo. All he had to do at night was pretend that his wife lying next to him was one of the nearby zebras, ponies, or llamas, all of them sweetly sleeping, and he himself would slip off easily into a deep furred sleep. The little girl, upon closer questioning, turned out to have just one wish for her tenth birthday: an entire box of fortune cookies to herself.

5.

Day after day: sun, clanging through the windows like a relentlessly cheerful succession of garish carillons, whether certain people liked it or not. "Keep working, and do not despair," wrote Brecht. Beware the voluptuousness of the demand curve. Happiness is a golden section. A lot of people seemed to like to go to the New York Public Library, establish themselves at a desk surrounded by books, and spend all afternoon stroking their smartphones.

6.

It wasn't that hard to walk through the city with the eyes of a developer, evaluating the organization of space according to maximization of profit. Or you could walk through the city with the eyes of a disappointed Romantic, that wasn't hard either, prizing a grassy empty lot bejeweled with dandelions, or a brick building caught in mid-ruin still faintly advertising "Coal." Nothing was very hard, when you came right down to it. Except sleeping.

7.

I never slept better in my life, the green-eyed veterinarian told us, than the years I lived across from a graveyard. In the evening my boyfriend and I would sit on our balcony with bottles of dark beer and drink in the deep peace emanating from the headstones, whose names had all been effaced by time. In India, a man opened a restaurant called "Hitler's," not realizing, he later said, that "Hitler" was anything more than a "famous European name."

8.

Sun, again. And again. There wasn't a single dress in the dresser. "Bureau" his dead mother had called it. "Chesterdrawer" they said in the South. His mother had larded their bureau drawers with bars of unwrapped perfumed soap. This was all long before he'd realized he felt most at home in airports. The girl was willing to share most of her possessions, but not, oh, not the box of fortune cookies, which she carefully stashed under her twin bed.

9.

A glass, a debt, an absolute ceiling. In truth, there were far more suitcases in the city than suits. "Summer afternoon," wrote Henry James, were the two most beautiful words in the English language. But for the heartbroken, the overworked, the underemployed, the grieving, and the lonely, "summer afternoon" was not two words but a sentence. And the schadenfreude they exuded on a cold and rainy July day hovered over the city like an extra layer of cloud.

TRANSACTION HISTORY 3

1.

In Europe around the turn of the last century, all upper-class boys were ceremoniously photographed wearing sailor suits. Now flea markets all over the continent overflow with little blue sailors who cannot save themselves. All up and down the diverted and straightened canal, some Romantic had once planted willows. Meanwhile, the lily flower had long since been abstracted into the fleur-de-lys.

2.

To a person, everyone she aimed her camera at would demur, "Oh, I'm really not photogenic." Which, when she thought more about it, could only mean that everyone thought they were better-looking than they really were. The covert exhibitionists liked to hang out in banks, on subway platforms, and in front of embassies, sneaking glances at surveillance cameras with their sexy gray shoulders.

3.

Das Leben ist kein Wunschkonzert. The rose had already glazed into the rose window. Was it a suitcase or a valise we watched slowly mounting the conveyer belt to be ingested by the belly of the jetplane, was it all just baggage, or was it maybe luggage? On their first date, he joked over a plate of pakoras, "I've got so much baggage by now, they no longer let me on airplanes." There was no second date.

4.

But with you, with you, I wanted to float lazily down the straightened canal under the non-native willows near stocked swans on a raft headed for the longest, lushest, plushest waterfall on record, the one we kept seeing over and over in the movies, and to plunge forever down its endlessly varying sameness. Panoramas of fakeness may have lost their cachet, but what you lost in me was more rarefied still.

5.

When a dance company opened a new performance space in a former soap factory, we were no longer impressed. When a bar owner shouted to us over electronica that here, chocolate had once been made, we yawned. We wished that the factories were still factories: we were hungry and dirty, we wanted bars of chocolate and of soap, something to suck on or take home to wash off our well-worn ennui.

6.

Despite all evidence to the contrary, we took it as a sign of the general psychic health of the populace that they thought they were better-looking than they really were. She collected photographs of boys in blue sailor suits — an ersatz, of course, but for what? The missing photograph of herself as a cowgirl? Das Leben ist kein Ponyhof. We all ought to have learned that, oh at the very least that, by now.

TRANSACTION HISTORY 4

I.

If ignorance is bliss, then happy people are by definition stupid. The melancholic had always *known* it, sitting at home nights organizing her collection of plastic owls. In the clock museum we learned that in schools, hospitals, and train stations there is one master clock and many slave clocks. The city at the bottom of the lake was like any other city at the bottom of a flooded lake: a mirror of our own desire to be drowned in insignificance.

2.

Was it meaningful that you were quick to tell me there was a term for the nineteenth-century swooning that occurred in the Uffizi and in front of Michelangelo's *David*, both men and women fainting to left and right before the dazzling marble body, but could not come up with the term itself? It was your birthday. The plastic owls had been manufactured to scare away other birds, as if wisdom itself were frightening — and indeed it was.

3.

It was not possible to go to a restaurant and not put something in your mouth. The coffee-table book was not on the coffee table, but in the bedroom splayed voluptuously across the bed. You felt old. What was I to make of our new neighbor's garden, resplendent with belladonna and nightshade, false indigo and foxglove, spurge and vetch? At the clock museum we read on a panel that, until around 1850, only the very rich could afford to tell time.

4.

One artist has painted more self-portraits than any other artist in history. The scruffy old man wearing a brown velvet jacket standing on the modernist bridge was asked what one piece of advice he would give to young people. "Don't bring owls to Athens," he answered, staring sadly down into the river. Watching him on TV, I wanted to bring him to the clock museum, the one place I could remember feeling I had most truly lost track of time.

5.

The city at the bottom of the lake haunted the solitary swimmer, who liked to imagine he could see the top of a drowned church steeple far down in the depths. Holding the jar of molasses, the melancholic, despite herself, started to think: if she could inoculate herself with black bile, might she be granted the occasional dose of ignorant bliss? As we looked and looked at clocks, we started to realize the clock-faces were also looking at us.

6.

The smoky glass oval in the velvet case was a Claude glass, through which city people on excursions used to turn the countryside picturesque. If we trained the Claude glass on the city, it would just remind us of how far we've fallen from the sweet ha-has of days gone by. The melancholic loved smoky ovals. In the clock museum you kept scoffing and insisting that all clocks are master clocks, since it is we who are the slaves of time.

TRANSACTION HISTORY 5

1.

If I hadn't seen it with my own eyes, I wouldn't have believed it: under the blue sky, a small steamroller imprinting the sand over and over with an advertisement for a jar of peanut butter. We had waited so long for summer, and all during that long, hot July and August we were still waiting. The woman with her hair full of hairpins drove cautiously down the hairpin curves to the town.

2.

The photograph of grains of sand magnified 200 times revealed microscopic works of art — gold, rose, opalescent scrolls, gaskets, sugars — where we had expected only a consoling beige monotony, the consoling beige monotony we always counted on when we came to the sea with our troubles to be consoled. Our troubles, too, were like artworks: constructed with love over time.

3.

Representations of the sea can have drenching effects on the landlocked. A room full of TVs showing a video of the ocean she accidentally walked into in an art museum in a landlocked land made her seasick — seasick like lovesick. If desire *does* spiral in nauseating waves, what are we to make of the erotic aporia of the sailor, who is always falling backwards from his decks into the sea?

4.

It is not possible to map a coastline, because the closer you zoom in, the more complexly intricate is the tracery of the coves and jetties, the sandbars all sliding off the map to be swallowed up by the great Undepictable. Each day at the beach we searched the sky for signs of summer, but all we saw were little airplanes towing banners exhorting us to enjoy an expensive brand of ice cream.

5.

As the melting chocolate case slid off my vanilla ice cream bar, you reached out a hand to rescue it, and the white clouds billowed for a moment over the rooftops. We wondered if the photograph of magnified sand grains was moving through the internet as it moved through our minds, called up and then abandoned, remembered and then forgotten, reified and liquidated. Just like our troubles.

6.

Even the napkins we had been given with the ice cream were printed with ads for a soft drink we'd never heard of. You said it couldn't hurt to buy just one to try it, and then I started an argument about your susceptibility to such siren songs. By the time we made it back to our spot on the beach, the peanut butter jars were gone, and the intoxicating monotony of the sand was at last incontrovertible.

TRANSACTION HISTORY 6

1.

She collected bits of wisdom and pinned them into specimen boxes in her mind to revisit whenever she felt like a fool, a fate which befell her far too often. Still, that summer there were satisfactions: People were archived in their apartment buildings at night, the museums stood suspended in their organized aesthetic arrest, and only the river moved through the city in the full liquidity of its argented indifference.

2.

As the society's machines got smaller and smaller, its buildings got taller and taller. Elevators rose and fell bereft of bellboys in the world's tallest skyscraper — which held the title only briefly, before a taller skyscraper on another continent knocked it off top spot. That day's wisdom: "Each day you have to abandon your past and accept it. And then, if you cannot accept it, you become a sculptor" (Louise Bourgeois).

3.

She glanced up on the subway and startled: in front of her was yet another clear plastic backpack — the girl's phone, wallet, lip gloss, and Tic Tacs visible to God and the world. It was an obscene scene; she wanted to throw her coat over it. And yet, because wisdom could appear at any moment, you had to be ready for it, like a butterfly-catcher carrying his net aloft as he threads through the skyscrapers of the city.

4.

The next bit of wisdom came from a movie: "Personne n'a vécu dans le passé, et
personne ne vivra dans le futur" (*Alphaville*). She pinned it. But had anyone ever actually lived in
the present? Wouldn't that be like having sex inside the clear plastic backpack? Foolishness
meant exposure, but borrowed bits of wisdom could cover you. Idle black train cars in a yard
blared MEGA COMBI MEGA COMBI MEGA COMBI.

5.

It was odd, how infinity pools were always pictured in architecture magazines with no
one swimming in them, how human blue merging into inhuman blue was never troubled by actual
humans. Pools were exposing, yet the water's distortion was protective. Then specimen boxes of
blue butterflies suddenly appeared in the shop windows, as if someone had not understood that it
is not the collection, but the collecting, that brings wings.

6.

He hoped to spare himself the indignity of not knowing what he could not possibly have
known. Knowledge was always antecedent, and too late. More than half the world's skyscrapers
have been built since 2000. Many have clear glass external elevators transporting tiny people up
and down their sides. Studies have shown that 20 percent are thinking of sex, 70 percent are
thinking of dinner, and 5 percent are thinking of clouds.

7.

It was all too easy to swim in the lake that summer without thinking about the fish chasing smaller fish chasing smaller fish along the bottom, to glide along the surface with one's refracted limbs and feel that one was "deeply experiencing" the lake. He pulled out the tiniest phone she'd ever seen. Bitter Lemon was the drink of choice; then there was a craze for homemade seltzer; then suddenly everyone had to have absinthe.

8.

The next specimen came from a website: "In einer Liebe suchen die meisten ewige Heimat. Andere, sehr wenige aber, das ewige Reisen" (Walter Benjamin). It was true: in love most people *were* looking for an everlasting home, not everlasting travel. But — why not both? An everlasting road trip in a homey van for two, stopping wherever you felt like to eat waffles, or to close the little curtains in back and fuck.

9.

For some the drink of choice was the choice to drink, night after night, themselves into an infinity pool of blissful stupor in which it emerged that the only solution to human foolishness was to merge into inhuman blue. Others chose the intoxication of order, and sat at home nights in their skyscrapers taxonomizing bits of wisdom. She slept badly beneath her blanket, for she dreamed that underneath her pillow shone the clear plastic backpack.

LANDSCAPE

AND

PORTRAIT

LANDSCAPE

(ADRIAEN VAN DE VELDE, GEMÄLDEGALERIE, BERLIN, MID-1600S)

The apotheosizing of an emptiness in three landscapes hanging in a room all depicting valleys, three hollows, all holding nothing but a fragility painted some also approximating a hollowly foxed golden sky

PORTRAIT

Five container ships crammed
with abandoned computer monitors
depart London at 3:55 p.m. bound
for Sri Lanka

ENZYKLOPÄDIE

DES

UNGESCHMACKS

.

ENZYKLOPÄDIE
DES UNGESCHMACKS 1

I.

She circled the vitrine labeled "Principles of False Design" in the design museum, eyeing the objects assembled there for ridicule — Victorian rose wallpaper and Chinese pagoda ashtrays, a faux-wood cuckoo clock — all of which she was troubled to find aesthetically pleasing. She opened her notebook to the list she was compiling of beautiful words for ugly things, and wrote down "effluvia."

2.

Vintage photographs revealed that what was now a plain stone plaza between two ornate banks in the historic district had, seventy years earlier, been a large, lush garden with gravel pathways, a series of pavilions, and a fountain gushing in its exact center. How disappointing that the garden was gone. Real estate agents sold "homes" and not "houses" anymore. "Cozy," everyone knew, meant small.

3.

He was startled to notice in an old guidebook that had sat unopened on his shelf for years that his train station, Hackescher Markt, used to be called Marx-Engels Platz. Cities were palimpsests. But the disturbing thing about palimpsests was that they were furtive. Lulled by surface into believing in the ex nihilo of surface, you were lulled into extirpating the layers of traces no eraser can erase.

4.

In the back room of the design museum was a traveling case whose dark green velvet
had been molded to hold examples of "good" design. A century ago, it was circulated
pedagogically in remote towns and schools. Zeal, it seemed, was a force in the universe that, like
lust, simply had to exhaust itself — in this case attaching parasitically to neat white milk pitchers
and futuristic looking forks.

5.

She didn't know what to do with the knowledge that the nondescript stone plaza had once
been a garden in twenty-seven variegating shades of green she would have taken beautiful
pleasure in strolling through. That the train station beneath his window used to announce a
disappointed ideology. She knew all about disappointment, though, oh yes — how it was like
interest, how it could compound.

6.

Deep down, surely everyone knew that real estate agents weren't really selling "homes," but
soon even architects could be heard discussing new developments of mixed-income "homes,"
and the news reported that the median price of new "homes" in the city was rising, with no end in
sight. Didn't the faux-wood cuckoo clock have a lesson to teach us about aspirations it didn't find
necessary to fulfill?

7.

On the opposite page there was a list of ugly words for beautiful things. The first entry was "pulchritude," the most recent "molding." The thing about disappointment was how disappointment piled on top of disappointment, like stories on a Chinese pagoda. An old painting he happened to see in a museum showed that the course of the river had once run straight through his apartment building.

8.

Mostly we did not believe that the city we loved was only a layer that would be replaced by other layers, that every building, every square, every garden had been traced and erased and retraced and re-erased. But at other times, lying on our feather beds at night, it was all we could do not to think about it. Did this knowledge make us smarter or more lovable, did it make us more beautiful, less disappointed?

9.

He told us, over coffee in a café that shortly thereafter became a bank, that he made his living as a "stager." This meant that he furnished houses for sale to make them look more like "homes"; for an outlay of $1,000, he said, you could put up the price $10,000. Not long after that, three more words were added to the list of beautiful words for ugly things: schadenfreude, crestfallen, farce.

ENZYKLOPÄDIE DES UNGESCHMACKS 2

1.

The house had been built in the 1930s, then renovated out of recognition in the 1960s, then re-renovated back to its original state in the 1990s, and finally demolished in 2008. Turning the pages of the picture book on German forests, he paused at a photo of a trophy room in a Bavarian castle hung floor to ceiling with stag horns, their blossoming Vs arranged in rows of repeated outbranching joy.

2.

It was a question that was circulating behind closed doors throughout the city those magnificent April days: Could hard currency get any harder? And you, your heart beat so fast the first time you kissed me I had to re-categorize the chest as the horn of the victrola, playing a record you may or may not have wanted me to hear. So many boys in your class wanted to grow up to be backwoodsmen.

3.

The snowflakes seemed to adhere to a spatial order as they fell, each snowflake spiraling equidistant from each other snowflake, as if they attracted and repelled each other at exactly the same rate. She couldn't stop thinking of a movie about killer bees she'd seen in the 1970s, in which, at the end, a woman lies down and allows her entire body to be covered by killer bees — not one of which stings her.

4.

All over, owners gasped as dropped popcorn ceilings from the 1960s were removed to reveal high ceilings from the 1920s, with egg-and-dart moldings. If taste is narcissistic, well then is tastelessness necessarily altruistic? When the narcissi were narcissistic, we too fell irreversibly in love with their image. It is spring!, she told the spatially ordered snowflakes falling all over everything. It is spring!

5.

The three-hundred-year-old Pennsylvania farmhouse was sold to a couple who promised to preserve it and then bulldozed everything except for one fireplace. Soon the banks were all giving soft loans. There were two kinds of people: those who cared too little, and those who cared too much. He hung a picture over his desk of the artists and architects who'd protested the amputation of Penn Station.

6.

O I wanted you to cover my entire body like a swarm of killer bees, though I wasn't at all sure that you wouldn't sting. Actually, let me revise that. Your heart beat more like the techno record our DJ neighbor played late in the night, a sped-up speed one's heart can't not respond to, troubled, in dumb involuntary empathy. I lost myself in the books arranged by color on your shelves, the majority red.

7.

Most passersby thought the bird silhouette stickers on the windows were decoration, when in fact they were meant to prevent the deaths of birds that cannot, until too late, perceive glass. Surely the stickers are bad taste: a confusion of intention and execution. What would it be like to be unable to perceive glass, to believe that transparency is transparent because it's hiding nothing, is truly true?

8.

But it was too late, too late — far too late to look at the antlers without having gone through all the historical stages — covetousness to outrage, to irony, to ironic outrageous covetousness like passing through a series of tunnels on a train. Even as we sat watching the sunset, somewhere a lamp was turning into an antique; somewhere a sofa was converting from bad taste to good taste.

9.

Come, I said to you from behind a wall of glass lined with bird stickers, come kiss me again, your mouth is a taste that is always in good taste. Destruction isn't the only attraction. Desire is liquid like glass, melting down centuries. The snow may try all it likes, it can't shut down the spring. Just ask the spatially ordered forsythia, blooming forth like a neat yellow rash on the edges of the forest.

ENZYKLOPÄDIE
DES UNGESCHMACKS 3

I.

On the center shelf of the "Encyclopedia of Bad Taste" was a square of blowzy rose-patterned wallpaper which, the text noted, was still a runaway success for the manufacturer to this day. In other words, the extent of the general benightedness was beyond the encyclopedists' worst nightmares. In the distance, two blackened church steeples rose above the trees like two black cat's ears.

2.

We heard that he had gone into the glazier's and ordered three new windows and a dozen donuts. The melancholic wished she could get what she wanted in life as effortlessly as a bee gets pollen from a flower. Shouldn't the objects of her desire also flock impassively in a field, beautiful and bursting with pollen, and defenseless? The result, she knew, would be righteous honey.

3.

Taste was so infantile anyway. As if "rational" adults could only judge the world like babies, sticking everything they got their hands on into their mouths. At the breakfast table, you snapped open the newspaper and read that yet another celebrity had been found asphyxiated in a hotel room from too much autoeroticism. If you lick a banana slug, it is said, your tongue goes numb.

4.

It seemed the equation could be made: the more sad plants in the office window, the more soul-eroding the job. A cluster of dusty Boston ferns and spider plants was like a wan green SOS. If the blowzy rose wallpaper is not to one's taste, one can just spit it out. The encyclopedists had a stash of volumes of Adolf Loos for palate cleansers. The melancholic ate a whole angel-food cake.

5.

There was the beautiful and then there was the sublime, but nowhere had anyone said anything about the tasteful. Was an Alp tasteful? Was a blowzy rose tasteful? After all, a great Russian dancer started out as the Golden Slave in the Kirov Ballet and ended up on *The Muppets*. The most elegant ice skater in the world decorates her apartment with hordes of hot pink teddy bears.

6.

We found it a bit amusing to imagine the encyclopedists hunched over their labor, collecting specimens of bad taste with proselytizing zeal to disabuse a public addicted to blowzy rose wallpaper and never to quit it. A bit amusing, and a bit bemusing. We liked blowzy roses — a bit. The word "bit" comes from "bite." Try as you might, there is no circumventing the human mouth.

LANDSCAPE

AND

PORTRAIT

LANDSCAPE

(PHILIPS KONINCK, GEMÄLDEGALERIE, BERLIN, MID-1600S)

The horizon pulled like taffy, pulled horizontally taut to the edges of the six canvases
around the room, the horizon pulled hypnogogically like taffy, golden taffy
pulled to each extreme, all horizontality, until the viewer appears like a vertical
admonishment, who would also like to be horizontal

PORTRAIT

A barge full of garbage departs New York City
bound for South Carolina, is not allowed
to dock, travels to Belize, is not
allowed to dock, is sent back
to New York City

55

FOUND TO BE

BORROWED FROM

SOME MATERIAL

APPEARANCE

FOUND TO BE BORROWED FROM SOME MATERIAL APPEARANCE 1

1.

She was reading a newspaper article about the Amber Room, stolen from Russia by the Nazis and found sixty years later buried in the Czech Republic, and thought of her own amber rooms, stolen by others and by herself, buried and never to be found throughout the Sudetenland of her body. The developers were inking deals, the ATMs were dispensing their usual neat stacks, the trams were depositing their pensive cargo all over the city.

2.

The most accurate chronometer in the sixteenth century? The hourglass. It was like the aftermath of a day at the beach: sand had gotten into everything, and for days afterward he kept finding it in his clothes, his hair, between the pages of his books. After the fall of the wall, they quickly buried the gigantic carved Lenin head in sand on the outskirts of the city. She sat down at her computer and typed in www.cabinetdecuriosites.com.

3.

How time spells itself out in gradations of green, aging centuries from early spring to late summer, fluorescent chartreuse April lawns darkening into bottle-green renunciations, late August oak leaves almost mahogany with the tarnishing concessions of the summer. Three star architects decided to join forces on a state-of-the-art planetarium. "People are basically good" is an American truism that Americans think is a universal truism.

4.

Over the years, the massive carved Lenin head was remembered from time to time, dug back up, put in a film or exhibition, and then reburied. When he published his new book, she saw that he had carefully excised all the dedications to her which had once sat atop many of the poems. Each day at three the man went and sat in the lobby of the Einstein Tower in Potsdam, hoping it was possible to absorb genius through genius loci.

5.

Time seemed to understand itself best in the tiny clock-repair shop he had to rush past every day in his haste to be on time for work. Night was falling, and the people all sat quietly in their living rooms, wondering if the future had any candy in its purse. And the next evening other people, people who had seemed intact as pomegranates, began spilling seeds of grief, loneliness, and despair all over the redeveloped plaza.

6.

They were so jumpy, those Indian summer days: he said "terrace" and they all heard "terrorist." They didn't know why the summer was "Indian." They knew that "boulevard" came from "bulwark." The trucks rumbled by all night, depositing construction materials at the new developments. Her husband hinted that her poems were too precious, so she wrote *fuck* in one, which her father discovered, and threw her book into the trash.

7.

The terraced mountains had nothing to tell us, the guard dogs let loose in the high-grassed paths troubled our luxurious little landscape studies. He read that the cash-strapped city was going to unbury the Lenin head for good and charge money to see it in a museum. At the dinner party she felt shy and thought of Cécile Sarkozy, who, when asked how she felt about moving into the Elysée Palace, remarked she was "bored stiff" by the idea.

8.

The water was so restful. It was the only thing that everyone that fucked-up summer could agree on. Nothing can be built on water, to the immense chagrin of the developers, masturbating in their offices to tinny new techno-pop, thinking up names like "Fox Hunter's Pointe" and "Inglewood Estates." Built based on the utopian principles of New Babylon, the Metastadt had fallen apart within fifteen years of its erection.

9.

The emotion bottling up in the champagne Marxist was either going to explode, skyrocketing him into the stratosphere, or sink him like a stone in his Gucci jeans. There were fates worse than being too clever by half, such as being insipid in spades. Or being a head buried and reburied in sand. We hated the developers, true, but that didn't mean as soon as we got any money we wouldn't buy the fanciest new apartment we could.

FOUND TO BE BORROWED FROM SOME MATERIAL APPEARANCE 2

I.

She wrote him a mental note: *If I dream about you every night, does that mean you have traumatized me?* Dream. Trauma. Dream. *Traum* (German). It paid to beware of the seduction of similarity, opening up deep after treacherous deep. But finger by finger, etymology removed centuries of kid gloves. Sometimes in her dreams she swam and swam through the past like a vast swimming pool filled with pale blue feathers.

2.

It was like crunching over a wintry sidewalk spilled with bits of pale blue glass, and looking at the Ford truck parked there with its smashed-out passenger window. Was this the Gesamtkunstwerk? There's no event without aftermath. The remains of the damaged church had long since been imploded, its structure refracted in clouds of dust. To destroy is violent and to construct is violent, but stasis has its violence, too.

3.

And as soon as the man came around the café in the evening shilling newspapers, then we remembered that our little world was only one of a profusion of worlds — a single bubble clinging to the great foam. *Le Monde. Die Welt.* How odd, the philosophy student said, it is to watch workmen in blue overalls using their bodies as human tools — digging, lifting, carrying, pounding — when we all once used our bodies so.

4.

The camera caught the imploded steeple in free fall, its neat chevrons indicating their own oblivion in clouds of dust. She wrote him another mental note: *While it's true that I dream of you every night, I don't think of you at all during the day. It's as if you were in my mind, sleeping there by day, emerging like a nocturnal animal at night. And as my diurnal animal wakes up and reaches for you, you have just gone to sleep.*

5.

The day felt like an out-of-focus eye chart, for which the right glasses were never going to be found. Dubo. Dubon. Dubonnet. The steeple collapsed. There were workmen in blue overalls everywhere one looked: scaling buildings, dozing off on the subway, buying beer and sausage in the corner store. She watched one disappear into a courtyard. The workmen were always disappearing, and at night they vanished completely.

6.

Aftermath after aftermath after aftermath. Each word was a vault containing the pale blue glass of its history. Similarity was the seed of its own destruction. It had been years — hadn't it? — since they had sat that night at the café wishing they were train conductors whose refusal to go to work would paralyze entire countries. And even if the letters on the eye chart had been read correctly, they wouldn't even have added up to words.

7.

Because the past is as fictional as the future, but better at masquerading as real. A workman's hand had fashioned the neat chevrons. At exactly that moment, the glass fell from her hand and shattered on the balcony. Her mind grew littered with pale blue mental notes. He went out for a walk to let the syntagmatic relationship of house to house soothe the agitation of the interchangeable fragments reconfiguring in his mind.

8.

In the library she found out that *trauma* and *dream* didn't have the same root after all. That night, her most traumatic dream was set in a handsome wood-paneled library. The steeple fell at an angle, its gold cross swallowed in clouds of dust. A damaged building must be further damaged, because damage attracts damage. There were workmen for hire to create, and workmen for hire to destroy, all wearing the same blue overalls.

9.

But how could a dream traumatize? If you said that, then you'd say a butterfly could dispense venom, or stasis could smash in a truck window, strewing the floor of your mind with bits of glass. Was stasis the most violent state? The mental notes piled up meaninglessly like crumpled eye charts. And that night, after she turned out the light, the past once again received her ceremoniously, with its pale-blue feathery arms.

FOUND TO BE BORROWED FROM
SOME MATERIAL APPEARANCE 3

1.

There were two words that for a long time she couldn't tell apart, despite all the index cards she wrote them down on and the mnemonic exercises she attempted: *Vernunft* and *Vergnügen*, reason and pleasure. She even tried to trick her mind into associating the letter "g" with pleasure, like the silent "g" in "sigh," like the sighs she made under her lover, who did not like to speak during sex.

2.

She knew accidentally saying "reason" when she meant "pleasure" was a bad idea, especially to the silent lover — but there the two words sat, marooned in acoustic shipwreck. In England, all swans are property of the queen. Watching the soccer game with his friends at a bar, he raised an eyebrow when he realized the music to "God Save the Queen" was the same as the music to "My Country 'Tis of Thee."

3.

It is said you must be exposed to a new word seven times before you can retain it. Only a few fragments of the speech emerging from the lecturer's mouth successfully penetrated his stupor, including "He was known for his beard, like Karl Marx" and the repeated word "Habibi." Habibi. Habibi. Habibi. Wasn't repetition an elixir? — A return promising a return that can only return altered, older, much older.

4.

For to "alter" is to age (älter: German, "older"). And though the lover's silence remained unaltered, underneath him she was altering, altering. Suddenly she noticed that *Vernunft* contained "*nun.*" Hadn't nuns abnegated pleasure? Weren't their habits reasonable? Pleasure carried within it the promise of unreasonable repetition. Habibi. Habibi. Swans repeated themselves unreasonably all over the canals.

5.

We wished that films still had a frame at the end that said "The End." We went to the movies hoping to leave altered — OK, we wanted *Vergnügen* more than we wanted *Vernunft*, we wanted to sink down into the drowsy liquid of the dark movie theater and pleasurably devolve into those deep-ocean fish with the dreamily phosphorescent eyes. To the reasonable, reason is pleasurable. And to the pleasurable —?

6.

Reason and pleasure, pleasure and reason. The reasonable Englishman wanted to own just one swan. Maybe she could think of the umlaut in *Vergnügen* as the unreasonably pleasurable bite marks of a silent lover. Later that night, he read on Wikipedia that the music to "God Save the Queen" was also the music for the national anthems of Russia, Switzerland, Norway, Denmark, Germany, and France. The End.

FOUND TO BE BORROWED FROM SOME MATERIAL APPEARANCE 4

1.

If you make a declaration of love under a waterfall, does anyone hear it? The anthropologist disdained the phrenologist, though he had one of those porcelain phrenology heads on his mantel. It took almost three years to dismantle the building. She was trying to get funding for a research project in which she would determine from exactly how many apartment windows in the city the TV tower, or even part of it, could be seen.

2.

That night we saw her again: the blonde girl who shuffled through the subway cars crying and begging, her scruffy dog clutched in a hug. Was she an actress, or truly a fellow damsel in distress? We were like vending machines that couldn't tell the difference between coins and slugs. Grief is only too real to the Madonna Lachrymae weeping in paintings and statues all over several continents, for those who know what real grief is.

3.

Years beforehand, the hammer-and-compass had been taken down from its pride of place on the façade. He'd read somewhere that all cathedrals are copies of other cathedrals, that all gardens are copies of other gardens. On Sundays he took the double-decker bus to get to the double-decker train, thinking his double-decker thoughts. He wanted to lie double-decker with his girlfriend, and have her pop out little copies of him.

4.

If you make a declaration of love on a freeway overpass at rush hour, does anyone hear it? In German *Glück* means both *luck* and *happiness*, like a golden Japanese cat waving its mechanical paw from the dark recesses of a store window at night, startling her on her way home from the subway. The word "maudlin" comes from Mary Magdalene, iconic weeper weeping through Catholic iconography all over the continent.

5.

Three years long the building was dismantled, piece by painstaking piece, till all that was left in the end was a lawn. Any anagram of *aesthetic* must include *ethics*. We gave the crying blonde girl coins or slugs. The anthropologist was a repressed aesthete, something he'd never admit to the phrenologist. Each day he attempted to tamp down his desire to have beauty at all costs — even, if necessary, the phrenologist's head.

6.

From their living-room window they could see the illuminated TV tower, and from their kitchen window, on the far side of the apartment, the illuminated cathedral. No longer were buildings allowed to simply lurk in the dark at night, keeping their own nighttime thoughts for themselves. If you made a declaration of love from the top of the TV tower down into the city on a windy afternoon, would anyone hear it?

7.

Each time we walked past the building being dismantled panel by panel, we saw time compartmentalized into pieces we didn't want to see, we felt the presence of an indecency, like weeping in public. After the breakup, he would sit in his apartment at night and wait for it: a dog barking alone somewhere, a few houses over, but in which direction he couldn't tell — maybe to the south of him, but also possibly to the north.

8.

Was it not possible, then, to be unhappy and yet lucky, or unlucky and yet happy? Happiness had long since been confined to totem moments in booths. For a time he'd believed that his sadness was the last remnant of his erstwhile empire, and so he'd clung to it like a drowning polar bear clinging to a piece of ice. The phrenologist scorned the ethnologist, who scorned the archaeologist, who scorned the psychologist.

9.

We felt that violence was a fitting end for buildings, as it was a fitting end for eras, for regimes, and for tears. The statues and paintings of weeping women were hurled down and shoved onto a pyre in the night, their tears turned bright orange by the flames. We looked out on the scene from our ogee windows, our translations laid out before us, waiting for the right word — and for luck or happiness, whichever turned up first.

FOUND TO BE BORROWED FROM
SOME MATERIAL APPEARANCE 5

1.

The divorced man sat at his desk pretending to work but really imagining getting stuck in an elevator with his ex-wife. His theory was as follows: forced to sit with him once more in close quarters for many hours, she would have no choice but to remember why she had once fallen so vertiginously in love. He looked at the clock on his computer, which did not tick and had no hands. The elevator is the safest form of transportation there is.

2.

The news from Japan was bad. The bad news from Japan had displaced the bad news from Wisconsin, which had displaced the good news from Egypt, which had displaced the bad news from England, which had displaced the good and bad news from Tunisia. The news from Japan was bad, but not bad enough not to be displaced by the news from Libya. Taken to Leningrad as a girl, the only thing she remembered was a golden peacock clock.

3.

All over the city, lobbies sat cool and mirrored and empty, with one untouched sofa in the corner offering an invitation to linger and rescinding it at the same time. If you looked closely at the mirrors, you could see that they were foxed. She kept walking into elevators with no button for the thirteenth floor. Over profiteroles at the socialist-chic restaurant, they determined after some discussion that the shattered mirror on the wall had been shattered deliberately.

4.

He was surprised to find out that the new language he was learning had only one word for both "history" and "story." It also had only one word for both "luck" and "happiness." All the guilt-ridden people sitting in therapy week after week, he thought, could really learn something from languages, which don't ever apologize for their deficiencies and their insufficiencies, for their omissions, obsessions, obscenities, flagrancies, fallacies, or farragoes.

5.

Was it true, as she'd read once in a book, that we find ticking clocks soothing because they remind us of our own ticking hearts? Sitting on the train in the sun they looked out the window and trembled with relief: there was so much left to watch, to buy, to click on, to show off, to want, to lick, to reject. But first, a Nescafé in a cup printed "Nescafé." Wearing an "I ♥ NY" T-shirt down the streets of New York, she finally felt sufficiently tautological.

6.

Hunched over her desk late at night downing cups of vending-machine coffee, the aspiring writer fantasized about getting stuck in an elevator with a famous critic. Forced to sit together in close quarters for many hours, they'd soon be making out on the cold floor and later, in fond reminiscence, he would offer to blurb her next book. The new language had no word for serendipity, none for jet-lag. It had no words for disoriented or sentimental.

7.

But wasn't it, at last, time? The grandfather clock ticking in the mirrored hallway "tells" time, as if time, too, were a story, and time *is* a story, it is a ghost story that keeps adults wide awake in their beds at night like children while snow falling outside renders the city sugary and skeletal. The doubled grandfather clock required two keys. In the hotel room, they turned on the TV looking for bad news and could find only an extended reportage on golf.

8.

It is hard to notice the orient in disoriented, reading a book in the occident in a room with an oriental rug. That was the winter that desires kept yawning open like elevator shafts into which people fell like black cats, falling down and down while universes all around expanded. It was a problem of geometry: desire was a part of her that was now and would always be greater than her. Remember the lesson of the elevator: welcome everyone, expel everyone.

9.

The activist fantasized about getting stuck in an elevator with the president. Forced to sit with the activist in close quarters for many hours, the president would listen to reason and at last decide to do something about deforestation. The people in the airport checking their phones for the time watched TV screens as the bad news from Japan was replaced by the good news from Tunisia. One by one their flights were called and they were lifted off into the sky.

FOUND TO BE BORROWED FROM SOME MATERIAL APPEARANCE 6

1.

It is eerie to pass a jewelry store window at night, with its collection of beheaded velvet necks and severed hands. He watched it on CNN, then Al Jazeera, then the BBC, then in his bathtub, then in bed. Laughing at a party with intriguing strangers, he could feel himself nailed further and further into a version of himself that was just one possible version. But soon enough, if he wasn't careful, it was going to be "him."

2.

You told me that Locke had compared the human mind to a printing press and to a camera obscura. I said my mind was sometimes like a stereoscope, sometimes like a zoetrope, sometimes just a misanthrope. We drove by the repurposed corset factory on our way to the old quarry renatured into a lake, and you put down your cigarette to ask, "When did a 'manufacturer' ever actually work with his hands?"

3.

On the far hill was an old brick factory with broken oval windows and chipped gingerbread trim. Faded letters spelled out SCHOKOLADENFABRIK, which made her reach for the consolatory dark chocolate bar in her pocket. It seemed like chocolate shouldn't have to be fabricated, that it should just occur in nature. Or at least be made not by humans but, like honey, by tiny single-minded workers with wings.

4.

In Leipzig a swarm of businessmen entered the train, all carrying identical briefcases and iPhones, all dressed in interchangeable dark suits. They were as schematized and majestic as hard currency, designed to pass smoothly through banks, wire transfers, and hands. He watched it on YouTube, clicking "Replay" over and over like a stoned mouse. He downloaded it onto his phone and watched it while idling at red lights.

5.

In truth, she'd always secretly found businessmen awfully erotic. She wanted to nestle her hair into their dark overcoats, to plunge her hands deep into the pockets of their neatly pressed pants. A businessman must always be clothed, for without his clothes he is no longer a businessman. The mind was also an X-ray machine, an ATM, a turntable, a movie theater with blue velvet curtains and a big glittering marquee.

6.

The hand that still resides in "manufacture" is not the invisible hand of the market, you told me — *not* the hand that feeds that ought not be bitten — *not* workers in rust belts handed pink slips — *not* hands cut off in factories where underpaid workers now work for underhanded new capitalists — not a lost world of meaning achieved through fingers. Rather, it is more like handsome, and handy, and hand-in-glove.

7.

But hands do still manufacture pleasure, you continued suggestively while your hands reached for the buttons on my coat. Seized by an irrepressible urge to bibliomance, I took down *Society of the Spectacle* from the shelf and read: "The spectacle aims at nothing other than itself." Chocolate shops were popping up all over the metropolis, for we weren't unique in our need to be reminded of the universe's fitful sweetness.

8.

It sure was soothing, how all the airplane's little cream movie screens unfurled from the ceiling at the same time. Yet somehow we disembarked and did not ever sit back, relax, and enjoy the flight. The mind was an Enigma machine, a lie detector, a television set with a rabbit antenna on snow. When she was seven, she'd been obsessed with her father's calculator-watch. He watched it to fall asleep and to wake up.

9.

There was a rumor circulating among the flora and fauna that, after they killed off the honeybees, humans would manufacture honey themselves, building honeycomb-like factories and pollinating flowers with their own two hands. Worried that the bulk of his accumulated experience now outweighed any hope for change in the future, he wandered into the derelict Schokoladenfabrik and watched it in the dark.

LANDSCAPE
AND
PORTRAIT

LANDSCAPE

(DIRCK VAN DER LISSE, GEMÄLDEGALERIE, BERLIN, MID-1600S)

The fetishization of nature in eight landscapes around a room is the fetishization of nature segmented into culture, nature deposited into frames at exactly that moment in the general segmenting when nature takes on the tragic dimension of culture, goldenly tamed

PORTRAIT

Two cruise ships full
of North Americans on holiday
round the Cape of Good Hope at 4 a.m.
dumping garbage along
the curve

SNOW

SERIES

S N O W S E R I E S 1

She thought that if she stared hard enough at the past, she might catch the moment when it turned into history. Or at least when it turned into happiness: like sugar crystallizing into sweetness in the mouth, the past crystallizing into pastness in the mouth of time, which crunches it into the petit-fours of history, recent history, ancient history. Across the valley, the apartment block kept bleaching in the sun.

*

It was with full cognizance of the worldwide melting of glaciers that we rode the téléphérique up to gaze down at the glacier at the top of an incognizant world. It looked like nothing more than a dirty ice-skating rink extending for miles, but still exuded the pathos of an expiring species, I said, when you leaned over and kissed me for, as only became clear later, what would be one of the last times.

*

In the shop window: a row of plaster copies of Mont Blanc, and underneath that a row of plaster copies of the Matterhorn. She sideswiped his grandfather's Cadillac just once on the dozens of dizzying hairpin curves down into the town. The Alps in the distance looked exactly like the Alps; the slices of cherry cake on white porcelain plates in the mirrored café looked exactly like slices of cherry cake.

She asked him why there was a chapel in the airport. He asked her why it made them so happy to go to museums to look at objects that used to belong to the filthiest of the filthy rich. By the time they made it to the zoo to see the famous baby polar bear, it had morphed into a big smudged adult with a protuberant snout and teeth that could gnash their bones into powder in the time it takes a snowflake to melt.

*

They knew there must be a warming point at which sentiment melts into sentimentality, pathos into bathos. Which Alp was framed in the window when the sun exploded on his grandfather's bed? Staring at the ice we saw a ring, which no carving with your pocketknife could deliver to my hand. Why, she wondered, aren't whole industries invested in trying to stop the present from deliquescing into the past?

*

Meanwhile, it said in the novel, *I had the voluptuous sensation of being slowly erased by the billowing steam of a nineteenth-century train* . . . She asked him why it was that the Italians call Germany Tedesco, and the French call it Allemagne. Brushing her ear with his lips, he asked her whether she thought that each of the gilded Louis XIV desk's dozens of locked drawers would open to only one gold key.

In the mirrors they watched the cherry cake slices recede into infinity. He kept talking about how the Swiss chalets back down in the village had looked exactly like Swiss chalets. She wanted to feel it, the instant the photoshopped photograph of a glacier turned into "art history," the whitewashed apartment block turned into "the vernacular," its recessed balconies noted in volumes on architecture.

*

For there must be an exact notch in time when it occurs: a building falls into a ruin, a ride on the téléphérique ices over into a memory, a distant memory freezes into a fetish, a loved one disappears over the horizon for good, like a container ship loaded with adult polar bears distributed to indifferent southern zoos. A video of the abandoned polar bear's death spiral has almost a million views on YouTube.

*

The only thing they could afford to order at the café was snow-capped hot chocolate. Years later, tucked into a copy of *The Castle*, she found an unsent postcard of the baby polar bear. Hadn't she only wanted him to lace up her ice skates and take her back up to the glacier? Hadn't she only wanted to skate and skate and skate until she could trace figure eights straight into the brown mountainous ground?

SNOW SERIES 2

There once was a polar bear who didn't know that he was a polar bear, because he'd been raised in a zoo by people. What would a polar bear have to know, to know that he was a polar bear? That's what the people would never know. All that winter, as we roamed around the gingerbread town, we kept noticing how the snowmen's bodies were segmented like insects', and how the new snows kept resembling other, older snows.

*

The beautiful young woman slowly realized that her beauty was a currency, but did not know how best to spend it. "It is difficult to be beautiful for long," wrote Max Jacob. The young woman read this and promptly forgot it. The Swiss chalets dotting the hillside did resemble other Swiss chalets. The polar bear who didn't know that he was a polar bear had snowy fur reflecting those regions where only our supercooled minds can go.

You were the one who wanted to ride the téléphérique all day long that winter, to float up over the Alps and then back down into the valley in an endless paternoster loop that would keep cycling us in and out of the sweetest ether. If "architecture is frozen music," then "music" must be "liquid architecture." The architecture itself was frozen: there were chalets trapped in aspics of ice. There were insects trapped in aspics of icicles.

*

In another city, people flocked to the zoo to imagine owning a baby polar bear named Flocke, whom they'd relinquish to her fate once she grew out of the phase in which they wished to crush her snowy soft fur with bear hugs. "Flocke" means "snowflake." No two snowflakes are alike. The wonder of uniqueness. The wonder of ownership. We opened our mouths to let unique snowflakes explode all over our wondering tongues.

Wonder upon wonder, tongue upon tongue, Alp upon Alp upon Alp. One Alp resembled another Alp. Gliding higher and higher on the téléphérique, we felt we were at last one with the Alps: encased in a glass eye floating up over the snow, all eye ourselves, our intertwining bodies architectonically segmented into distance, ownership, and desire. The glacier below us was beautiful, beautifully, violently expiring.

*

But later, as we moved deeper into winter, I couldn't help noticing how your body was starting to resemble a snowman's — it kept melting to nothing when I tried to hold it close. The old man wondered aloud why some valleys fill with water and become lakes, and others remain simply valleys. Eventually the young woman would know that beauty's currency was like any other: useless if hoarded, gone when spent.

SNOW SERIES 3 (AFTER AN ARTWORK BY HANS-PETER FELDMANN)

We heard about an artist who sent invitations to an exhibit that didn't exist, but we insisted that the exhibit had existed, for it had flared briefly in our minds before we were forced to extinguish it carefully. True, we were made of the same star matter as history, but wasn't it the kind of history that dissolves like snow in spring? Snow that looks architectural, but that no one remembers come summer.

*

She looked at herself in the mirror and saw a mourning dove looking back. Wasn't suffering supposed to make me wiser?, she thought. But she felt less and less wise. Whether the spring was a new spring or the return of a preexisting spring was a matter to be settled by the snowing pear petals. In the big city for the first time, the young man kept ending up at exhibits of sculpture made from garbage.

As glaciers all over the world went into accelerated melting, crowds of people stepped on accelerators to get to the zoo to coo at the baby polar bear who reigned there melting hearts. The polar bear sat ensconced in the fur of its own fate. We were riding the téléphérique, which whisked us up the valley, the valley above the valley, above another valley — into which the mountain, if it toppled over, would fit.

*

Oh we knew that less was more, but what dismayed us was that more must thus also be less. Had the exhibit existed? In a reckless moment we could even say that the snow falling all over our upturned faces existed, that garbage existed. In the zoo store, people bought stuffed doubles of the bear they'd eventually stuff into the trash. Her suffering felt architectural, but she told herself it, too, would dissolve in spring.

Why are there no right angles on airplanes, the math student wondered. Curve after curve on the seats, armrests, tray tables, portholes, tracing the curvature of the earth. The valley was an optical illusion, a trompe l'oeil, a gestalt figure — like the nonexistent art exhibit. And like suffering? The vase consumed the profile which consumed the vase which consumed the profile — neither of which existed.

*

Was any winter a new winter, or just the return of all the old winters, like how garbage always returns, how there is star matter even in trash? Once the baby polar bear was no longer a baby, the visitors melted away. She thought she saw a stuffed polar bear in a dumpster as they rose and rose in the téléphérique. A black comb on a white shelf, or a white comb on a black shelf? The only certainty was tines.

NOTES

In the weaving of some so-called "oriental" carpets, there is a phenomenon called "abrash" in which colors are imperfectly matched due to the diameter size of the fibers and small dye lots. These imperfections have sometimes intentionally been woven in to signify the imperfection of humans as opposed to the perfection of God.

"Enzyklopädie des Ungeschmacks" refers to a vitrine in the Museum der Dinge, Berlin, in which manufactured objects that supposedly offend good taste are on display. Related is the "Principles of False Design" exhibition in the Victoria and Albert Museum in London, curated in the 1850s by Richard Redgrave and Henry Cole.

The phrase "Found to Be Borrowed from Some Material Appearance" is taken from a passage on etymology in Emerson's essay "Nature": "Every word which is used to express a moral or intellectual fact, if traced to its root, is found to be borrowed from some material appearance. *Right* means *straight*; *wrong* means *twisted*. *Spirit* primarily means *wind*; *transgression*, the crossing of a *line*; *supercilious*, the *raising of the eyebrow*."

ACKNOWLEDGMENTS

Some of the poems from these series were originally published, sometimes in earlier versions, in the following journals: *Better Magazine, Black Warrior Review, Denver Quarterly, Faultline, Gulf Coast, Jubilat, Loose Change, No Man's Land, Pallaksch. Pallaksch, Shearsman, Wave Composition, Web Conjunctions, With+Stand,* and *Witness.* I'm grateful to the editors.

I am also grateful for fellowships to the Djerassi Resident Artists Program, the Millay Colony, and the Dora Maar House in Ménerbes, France, for time and space in which to work on this manuscript.

Thank you, as always, to my generous and invaluable friends who are also my readers. Special thanks and love to John Nijenhuis, not least for patiently reading the entire manuscript aloud to me over the course of one cold winter. My deep gratitude, as well, to Mark Levine and Emily Wilson.

KUHL HOUSE POETS

Christopher Bolin
Ascension Theory

Christopher Bolin
Form from Form

Shane Book
Congotronic

Oni Buchanan
Must a Violence

Michele Glazer
On Tact, & the Made Up World

David Micah Greenberg
Planned Solstice

Jeff Griffin
Lost and

John Isles
Ark

John Isles
Inverse Sky

Aaron McCollough
Rank

Randall Potts
Trickster

Bin Ramke
Airs, Waters, Places

Bin Ramke
Matter

Michelle Robinson
The Life of a Hunter

Vanessa Roveto
bodys

Robyn Schiff
Revolver

Robyn Schiff
Worth

Sarah V. Schweig
Take Nothing with You

Rod Smith
Deed

Donna Stonecipher
Transaction Histories

Cole Swensen
The Book of a Hundred Hands

Cole Swensen
Such Rich Hour

Tony Tost
Complex Sleep

Pimone Triplett
Supply Chain

Nick Twemlow
Attributed to the Harrow Painter

Susan Wheeler
Meme

Emily Wilson
The Keep